The Undercover Mathematician

T0328021

Contents

Written by Rachael Davis
Illustrated by Alice Negri

Collins

1 Sophie Germain

Have you heard of Sophie Germain?
Not many people have.

Sophie was born in Paris, France on 1st April 1776.
Girls were not allowed to learn subjects like Maths
at that time. But Sophie loved numbers and she was
determined to do what she loved.

Sophie went undercover to learn Maths in secret,
using a boy's name as a code name.

Sophie Germain

Have you heard of the Eiffel Tower? Lots of people have.

The Eiffel Tower is a famous building in France and Sophie is part of the reason it exists. During her lifetime, Sophie made **mathematical** discoveries about how objects **vibrate**. Her findings were very important in the construction of the Eiffel Tower.

Did you know?

The tower is made of 7,300 tonnes of iron. That is about the same weight as 2,000 female elephants!

Did you know?

The Eiffel Tower took two years, two months and five days to build.

the Eiffel Tower in Paris, France

Making sure a building like the Eiffel Tower doesn't fall over is hard. It uses a lot of **complex** Maths and Science.

The names of 72 scientists, engineers and **mathematicians**, whose discoveries helped build the Eiffel Tower, are **inscribed** on the building. The names are written in golden capital letters, 60 centimetres tall.

LE CHATELIER   BERTHIER   BARRAL   DE DION   GOUIN   JOUSSELIN   BROCA

Sophie's name is not inscribed on the tower. In fact, no women are included at all.

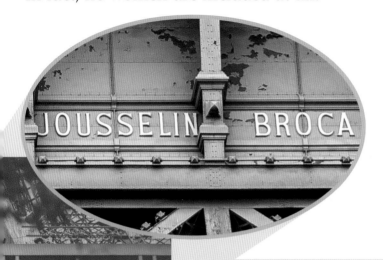

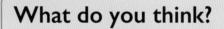

What do you think?

Why might Sophie's name have been left off the Eiffel Tower?
– by accident
– because she was a woman
– she didn't deserve to have her name on the tower

Even after people knew Sophie was amazing at Maths, she didn't always get the respect she deserved because she was a woman.

2 Sophie's childhood

Sophie Germain as a child

Sophie lived with her parents and two sisters in an apartment above the family's shop. Her father sold **silk** and made enough money for the family to live a comfortable life in Paris. When Sophie was 13, the French Revolution began.

Paris was a dangerous place during the French Revolution and so Sophie had to stay indoors. She liked reading in her father's library.

What was the French Revolution?

For a long time, a small number of rich people ruled France. A lot of people in France were poor and didn't have enough money for food. The poor people didn't think this was fair and fought against the rich and powerful people.

The French Revolution took place between 1789 and 1799.

The Bastille was a prison about one kilometre from Sophie's home.

The people of Paris attacked the Bastille during the French Revolution.

Paris during the French Revolution in 1789

7

One day, when Sophie was in her father's library, she read about a famous mathematician called Archimedes. Two thousand years ago, Archimedes was killed by soldiers for trying to protect his mathematical work. Sophie couldn't believe it! She decided anything that was worth dying for must be worth **studying**. From that day on, Sophie loved Maths and learnt as much as she could.

$$\sum_{n=0}^{\infty} 4^{-n} = 1 + 4^{-1} + 4^{-2} +$$

Name: Archimedes

Born: around 287 BCE

Died: around 212 BCE,
aged 75

Nationality: Greek

Maths skills:
He famously studied shapes and also invented a special screw. The "Archimedes screw" could pump water up to higher ground.

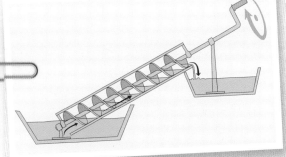

Sophie couldn't go to school and she didn't have a tutor to help her. The only way Sophie could learn about Maths was to teach herself from books. That can't have been easy. To make things even harder, Sophie's parents didn't want her to learn Maths!

Sophie had no choice but to learn about Maths in secret.

Late at night, when Sophie's family were all asleep, Sophie would read books about Maths in her bedroom. Her parents were horrified! They tried everything they could to make her stop. They put out the fire in her room so it was too cold and dark to study. But Sophie did not give up. She wrapped herself up in her blanket and carried on studying Maths by the light of a lamp.

One night, Sophie's room was so cold that her **inkwell** had frozen solid! When her parents discovered her the next morning, asleep at her desk, they realised Sophie was prepared to study Maths at any cost. Sophie's parents finally agreed to support her choice to study Maths. But she still had to teach herself from books, without the help of a tutor.

3 Sophie's code name

By the time Sophie was 18, she needed more advanced Maths books than the ones in her father's library. A new **university** called École Polytechnique had just opened in Paris. Sophie knew it was the perfect place to continue her studies. But there was a problem.

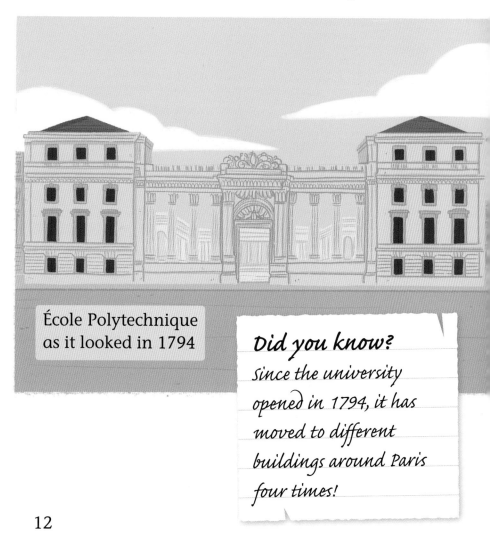

École Polytechnique as it looked in 1794

Did you know?
Since the university opened in 1794, it has moved to different buildings around Paris four times!

What do you notice about this picture of a university **lecture**?

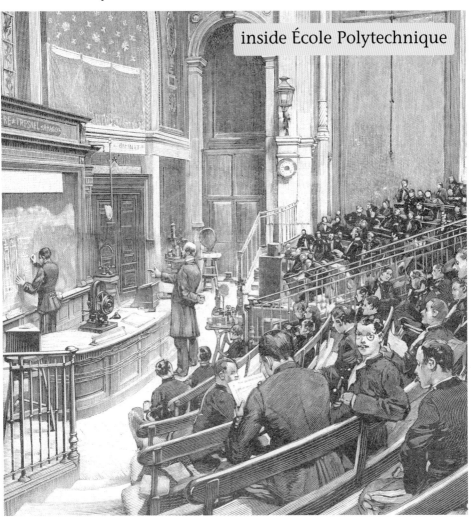

inside École Polytechnique

Only men were allowed to study at the university.

Once again, Sophie had an obstacle in her way. But she didn't let that stop her.

No one knows exactly how they met, but Sophie became friends with a young man studying at the university. His name was Antoine August Le Blanc. He agreed to share his lecture notes with Sophie.

Their plan was working well until …

Le Blanc had to join the army and was called away to war. Sophie wanted to keep studying, but how?

Sophie needed a new plan – a clever plan.

Sophie began to secretly collect Le Blanc's lecture notes from the university. She even started doing his homework, pretending to be him!

Sadly, Sophie's friend Le Blanc never returned from the war. And the name "Le Blanc" became Sophie's secret code name.

Everything was going well. In fact, everything was going too well. One of the university **professors**, called Joseph-Louis Lagrange, was so impressed with the homework Sophie **submitted** that he wanted to meet Le Blanc!

Was Sophie's cover about to be blown?

Name: Joseph-Louis Lagrange

Born: 25th January 1736 in Italy

Died: 10th April 1813 in France

Nationality: Italian-French

Maths skills:

He discovered new ways to solve equations. Equations are complex number sentences.

4 Sophie's mentor

Lagrange came to Sophie's home. He was shocked to discover Le Blanc was a code name and Sophie was a woman. But he didn't mind. In fact, Lagrange offered to become her **mentor**.

Sophie could now choose to learn about all the different parts of Maths and Science. She still loved numbers and patterns, particularly prime numbers.

Sophie learnt all she could about prime numbers, and she discovered new things about prime numbers that no one else knew!

Prime numbers are a set of special numbers than can only be divided by themselves and one to give a whole number. Seven is an example of a prime number:

$7 \div 1 = 7$

$7 \div 7 = 1$

7 can't be divided by any other numbers so 7 is a prime number.

Question: Can you think of other prime numbers?

Answer: 2, 3, 5, 7, 11, 13, 17, 19

Lagrange introduced Sophie to the other male mathematicians. But it was still difficult for her to join in. Not everyone was welcoming, and Sophie was incredibly shy.

a group discussion at the university

Sophie still could not officially attend Maths lectures.

What do you think?
Why didn't the male mathematicians welcome Sophie?

When Sophie was 25, a German mathematician called Carl Gauss wrote a new book all about numbers and patterns. Gauss was thought to be the most gifted and famous mathematician in Germany.

Name: Carl Gauss

Born: 30th April 1777

Died: 23rd February 1855

Nationality: German

Maths skills:
Gauss was a child genius. He helped his father with Mental Maths from the age of three.

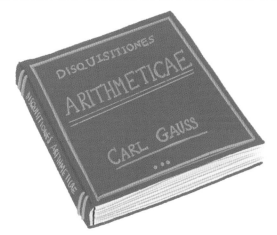

5 Letters to Gauss

Sophie really wanted to talk to Gauss about his work on numbers, but she still felt shy talking to other mathematicians. She decided to write to Gauss using her secret code name, Le Blanc.

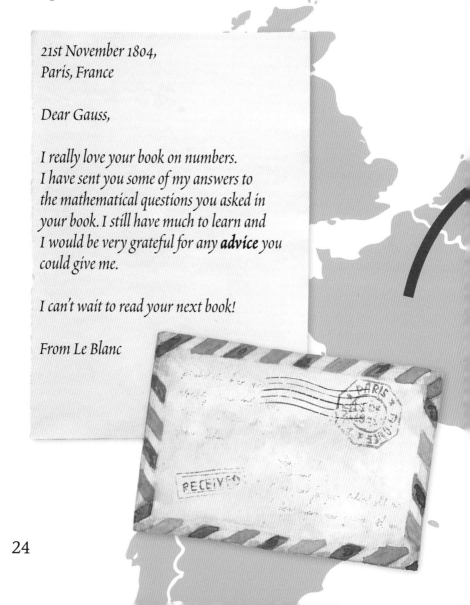

21st November 1804,
Paris, France

Dear Gauss,

I really love your book on numbers.
I have sent you some of my answers to
the mathematical questions you asked in
your book. I still have much to learn and
I would be very grateful for any **advice** you
could give me.

I can't wait to read your next book!

From Le Blanc

16th June 1805,
Brunswick, Germany

Dear Le Blanc,

I was delighted to receive your letter
and the mathematical answers you
sent me. Your work on prime numbers
is excellent. I am pleased to have made
a new friend who is so good at Maths.

From Gauss

Gauss was right. Sophie's work on prime numbers was excellent. Sophie would go on to solve part of a mathematical puzzle that had stumped mathematicians for two **centuries**. It was called "Fermat's Last Theorem".

While Sophie didn't find a complete solution to the puzzle, it was a huge achievement and showed how talented she was.

Fermat's Last Theorem was eventually solved around 190 years later in 1994 by Professor Andrew Wiles. Here is Wiles presenting part of his solution at Cambridge University.

Sophie and Gauss continued to write letters to each other. Gauss even wrote a letter to his friends about how impressed he was by Le Blanc.

I have been exchanging letters with a young mathematician from Paris, called Le Blanc. He is studying complex Maths and has sent me some great answers to the mathematical questions in my book.

Gauss had no idea that Le Blanc was Sophie's secret code name.

But it wasn't long before Sophie's cover was blown again!

Napoleon Bonaparte crowned himself Emperor of France in 1804. He fought most of Europe until 1815, including the German state where Gauss lived. Sophie became scared for Gauss. She remembered the story of Archimedes she had read as a child in her father's library. What if Gauss was killed by soldiers for protecting his mathematical work? She couldn't let that happen.

Napoleon Bonaparte

Sophie knew a general in Napoleon's army and asked him to check that Gauss was alive and well.

The general did as Sophie asked. Gauss was fine but very confused.

"But I don't know anyone called Sophie," Gauss told the general. "Why would a French woman care about me?"

Sophie knew the time had come to tell Gauss the truth. She had to reveal her true identity.

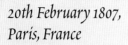

20th February 1807,
Paris, France

Dear Gauss,

I was so glad to hear you are fine! The general said you were confused why someone called Sophie cared about you. So, I must now tell you the truth. You do not know me as Sophie, but you do know me. Having grown up fearing being teased for being a female mathematician, I sometimes use the code name, Le Blanc. I hope knowing I am a woman does not change things and we can still be friends and talk about Maths.

From Sophie

30th April 1807,
Brunswick, Germany

Dear Sophie,

Thank you so much for asking the general to make sure I was fine during the war.

I am amazed to discover you are a woman! It is rare to find a person who loves Maths as much as I do. But to find a woman who loves Maths as much as me is even more incredible. There are so many obstacles that stop women from studying Maths. So, for a woman to fight for her right to study Maths, she must have the most noble courage, extraordinary talent and superior genius!

I would love to stay friends and continue talking about Maths.

From Gauss

6 Eyes on the prize

A year later, when
Sophie was 32, she saw
an extraordinary experiment.
A German scientist called
Ernst Chladni put some
sand on a plate of glass.
He rubbed a violin bow
on the edge of the plate.

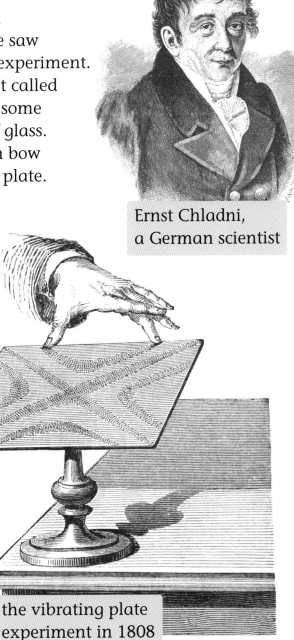

Ernst Chladni,
a German scientist

the vibrating plate
experiment in 1808

As everyone expected, this made the plate vibrate, creating different musical notes.

But what they didn't expect, was to see the sand form patterns on the plate. It was like the sand was dancing on the plate!

Chladni had uncovered a secret pattern of vibrations that no one knew how to explain.

different patterns made by sand on the vibrating plate

The experiment amazed all of France, including Napoleon. Napoleon told the French Academy of Sciences to offer a prize to anyone who could come up with a mathematical equation to explain the pattern of vibrations by 1812.

The prize was a gold medal made from one kilogram of gold.

the French Academy of Sciences in 1828

Sophie spent the next two years trying lots of different ways to solve the mathematical puzzle. This was her chance to show that women could be mathematicians.

In 1811, Sophie submitted an entry to the competition. She stopped using her secret code name Le Blanc and used her own name proudly. Finally, Sophie began to grow in confidence.

Surprisingly, Sophie was the only person to enter the competition! No one else had come up with an answer. But that didn't mean she would win; her entry still had to be right ...

Several months later, Sophie received bad news. She had not won the prize. The judges agreed that Sophie had come up with a good way to solve the puzzle, but she had made mistakes.

Sophie had shown her natural ability for Maths, but without a tutor to teach her the latest methods to solve Maths puzzles, she had made errors. Once again, having to teach herself Maths had held her back.

But Sophie didn't let this disappointment stop her. The competition deadline was extended to 1813 and, as always, Sophie **persevered**. She listened to all of the comments of the judges and was determined to make her entry better.

Sophie's second entry tried to solve the puzzle in a new way. The judges considered her entry. But it was bad news again. This time, Sophie had found the right answer, but she had made mistakes in explaining why the answer was correct. The judges were impressed, but they didn't award her the prize.

The competition deadline was extended again for a third and final time, until 1815. This was Sophie's last chance. She had already spent four years trying to solve this mathematical puzzle and she wasn't going to give up now.

Sophie tackled the problem one last time, using everything she had learnt and all her determination. Sophie submitted her third entry. Would she finally win?

RECHERCHES

SUR LA THÉORIE

DES SURFACES ÉLASTIQUES;

AB M^ELLE SOPHIE GERMAIN.

———

PARIS,
Mme Ve COURCIER, LIBRAIRE POUR LES SCIENCES,
RUE DU JARDINET-SAINT-ANDRÉ-DES-ARCS, N° 12.
1821.

Sophie's final entry

7 Sophie's success

Sophie did win!

Sophie had shown that even though she wasn't allowed to go to university like male mathematicians her age, she was just as good at Maths!

What do you think?

– What other things, even more amazing, could Sophie have done, if she had been allowed to go to university?
– What did Sophie gain by NOT being allowed a formal education?

It took more than just mathematical ability to win the Academy of Sciences prize. It was Sophie's determination and perseverance that helped too.

Sophie had to fight for her right to study Maths all through her life. She never gave up. When her first entry didn't win the competition, Sophie kept on trying.

In 1823, when Sophie was 47 years old, she was finally allowed to attend lectures at the Academy of Sciences as a mathematician. It was the first time a woman had been recognised as a mathematician by the Academy of Sciences. Sophie continued studying Maths until she died in 1831, aged 55.

Sophie's prize-winning work on vibrations was the beginning of a new area of Maths on **elasticity** and it is used to help construct buildings such as the Eiffel Tower. Her name might not have been put on the building, but mathematicians today know and value Sophie's Maths.

Sophie Germain

Sophie Germain began as an undercover mathematician, but her amazing talents are no longer secret.

As a result of her excellent work on Fermat's Last Theorem, a set of prime numbers have been named after her, called the "Sophiens".

There is a road and a school named after Sophie, in Paris, as well as a statue in her honour.

Sophie Germain school   Sophie Germain road

Today, both men and women study together at
the university, École Polytechnique.

École Polytechnique in Paris

Women have been allowed to study at
the university since 1972.

Sophie Germain is one of the greatest female mathematicians who has ever lived. She showed the world that it doesn't matter if you are a boy or a girl, Maths is for everybody and everyone can do it.

Glossary

advice suggestion of ways to help

centuries one century is 100 years. Two centuries is 200 years

complex something with lots of parts

elasticity the amount a building or object can bend and stretch

inkwell a pot of ink

inscribed wrote words onto an object

lecture an educational lesson taught at a university

mathematical something that relates to Maths

mathematicians people who do Maths

mentor someone who knows a lot about a subject and gives advice to someone who knows less about that subject

persevered determined to finish something difficult

professors the most senior teachers in a university

silk a light, soft material used to make clothes

studying learning a subject through reading books, or being taught by a teacher

submitted handed in something to be assessed

university a place to study at a high level, usually starting at age 18

vibrate move quickly to and fro

Index

Sophie Germain's life

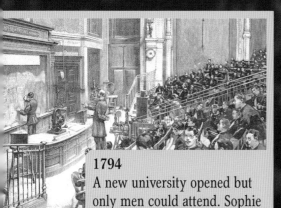

1794
A new university opened but only men could attend. Sophie became friends with Le Blanc.

1795
Sophie submitted work to Lagrange using the code name Le Blanc. Her real identity was discovered, and Lagrange became her mentor.

1776
Sophie was born.

1770   1780   1790   1800

1789
During the French Revolution, Sophie read about Archimedes and fell in love with Maths.

1804
Sophie wrote to Gauss using her code name Le Blanc.

1806
Gauss discovered Sophie's true identity.

1811
Sophie entered the Academy of Sciences' competition but didn't win.

1808
Sophie saw Chladni's vibrating plates experiment.

1831
Sophie died.

1889
The Eiffel Tower was completed.

1820   1830   1840   1890

1813
Sophie entered the competition again but didn't win.

1815
Sophie entered the competition a third time and she won!

RECHERCHES

SUR LA THEORIE

DES SURFACES ÉLASTIQUES:

ᴘᴀʀ Mᴸᴸᴱ SOPHIE GERMAIN.

PARIS,

Mᵐᵉ Vᵉ COURCIER, LIBRAIRE POUR LES SCIENCES,

1821.

1823
Sophie was allowed to attend lectures at the Academy of Sciences.

47

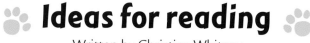

Ideas for reading

Written by Christine Whitney
Primary Literacy Consultant

Reading objectives:
- be introduced to non-fiction books that are structured in different ways
- listen to, discuss and express views about non-fiction
- retrieve and record information from non-fiction
- discuss and clarify the meanings of words

Spoken language objectives:
- participate in discussion
- speculate, hypothesise, imagine and explore ideas through talk
- ask relevant questions

Curriculum links: Mathematics: Number and place value; Writing: Write for different purposes

Word count: 2942

Interest words: centuries, lecture, mentor, persevered, prime numbers, vibrate, vibrations

Resources: Paper and pencils

Build a context for reading
- Ask children to suggest activities, events or jobs which do not allow women. Are there any? Was it always so?
- Before the children see the book, ask them what they understand by the word *undercover*. Explain to children that it is a compound word. Show the book and ask children to suggest reasons why the person on the cover might be an *Undercover Mathematician*.
- Now turn to the back cover and read the blurb. Sophie is very good at Maths. Ask children to predict what the problem is when she wanted to meet people.
- Introduce the words *centuries, lecture, mentor, persevered, prime numbers, vibrate, vibrations*. Ask children to work in pairs to suggest a sentence which uses one of these words correctly.

Understand and apply reading strategies
- Turn to the contents page and read through the different chapters in the book. Tell children that a book about someone's life is called a biography. Ask for volunteers to say which section they are most interested in reading and why.